Digitizing Dreams

Power of Dreams in Digital World

Ghoshak

Made with ♥ on the Notion Press Platform

www.notionpress.com

Disclaimer

"This book contains inspirational stories of entrepreneurs who have built their businesses through digitization. While the stories are based on real experiences, they are a combination of multiple entrepreneurial journeys, merged to create a cohesive narrative for informational and motivational purposes.

The authors and publishers do not claim any ownership or copyright over the events or concepts described. Any resemblance to other published works, real individuals, or businesses is purely coincidental and unintentional. The content is not meant to infringe on any copyrights, trademarks, or intellectual property rights.

The views and experiences shared in this book are those of the individuals featured and do not necessarily reflect the opinions of the authors or publishers. Readers are encouraged to conduct their own research before making business decisions based on the information provided".

Contents

Foreword

When the founders reached out to me requesting me to write this foreword for "DIGITIZING DREAMS," my mind travelled back to the day when I reviewed the Incubation application for Ghoshak. After going through over 100 application, my eyes were tired and my mind was reading everything on auto-mode. But with Ghoshak there was something different and I wanted to meet them immediately. I still recall how I was deeply impressed of their vision – unlike other applicants, they were not just another startup chasing valuations, the founders genuinely showed a deep-rooted desire to transform lives in India's heartland through digital empowerment. We wanted to extend our support and join them in this mission.

The ten remarkable stories captured in these pages – from Latha's journey of transforming her traditional saree business into a digital success, to the revolutionary urban kirana that reimagined local grocery, to the innovative fresh produce delivery venture – each represents a unique facet of India's digital transformation. These aren't just business narratives; they're testament to the often-overlooked reality that innovation doesn't always wear a suit or occupy gleaming office towers.

What makes this book particularly compelling is its raw authenticity. Having mentored the Ghoshak team through their early days, I witnessed their unwavering commitment to understanding the real challenges faced by small businesses. Whether it was helping a traditional kulfi maker embrace modern delivery systems, enabling an aluminium craftsman to reach global markets, or digitizing a legacy electronics store, their approach wasn't to impose technology, but to adapt it to fit within the cultural and operational fabric of these businesses.

The stories here represent the 3,000+ businesses transformed through digitization – and they aren't just success metrics for a startup. From the local perfume maker who digitized his ancient family recipes to the mesh manufacturing pioneer who revolutionized his industry, each story represents real families whose lives have been enhanced, communities that have been uplifted, and dreams that have found wings through technology.

This book arrives at a crucial juncture in India's digital transformation journey. While much has been written about India's unicorns and tech giants, the real revolution is happening in its small towns and villages, led by entrepreneurs who are embracing technology not for its novelty, but for its ability to create tangible value in their daily operations.

For aspiring entrepreneurs, this book serves as a masterclass in building with purpose. For policymakers and industry leaders, it offers invaluable insights into the real needs and aspirations of India's MSME sector. And for anyone interested in India's digital journey, it provides a ground-level view of how technology, when appropriately contextualized, can be a powerful force for positive change.

The stories shared in these pages remind us that true innovation isn't about disruption for disruption's sake – it's about empowerment, enablement, and creating lasting impact. Ghoshak's journey embodies this philosophy, and their success in digitizing dreams across India's diverse landscape is a testament to the power of purpose-driven entrepreneurship.

As you turn these pages, you'll find more than just business cases; you'll discover the beating heart of India's digital revolution, pulsing through its small towns and villages, one business at a time.

Prasad Menon CEO, CIBA

Acknowledgment

I extend my heartfelt gratitude to my grandfathers, Mr. C. Krishna Moorthy and S. Srinivasan, who inspired in me a deep commitment to helping entrepreneurs grow; to my parents, for their unwavering encouragement to pursue my passion; and to my wife, daughter, and son, for their endless patience and support as I dedicated long hours to my work.

A special thanks to Mr. Rajesh, Founder and CEO, and the entire Ghoshak team for giving me the opportunity to interact with so many inspiring entrepreneurs and for allowing me to share my own experiences with them. Your trust, support, and belief in my vision have meant a great deal to me.

I would also like to sincerely thank the entire Ghoshak team for their remarkable performance.

Thank you all for being pillars of strength and inspiration.

With Love & Regards,
TJ

Introduction: Digitizing Dreams

In the vast and vibrant tapestry of India's entrepreneurial landscape, there exists an uncelebrated league of heroes—small business owners from remote corners of the nation. At Ghoshak, we fondly call them digital warriors. They are the resilient torchbearers of India's digital revolution, transforming not just their own businesses but also the communities they serve.

These unsung entrepreneurs carry within them the essence of India's rich cultural and economic diversity. From bustling markets in small towns to serene villages tucked away in the countryside, they operate in spaces where challenges often outweigh opportunities. Yet, it is in these spaces that innovation thrives, and resilience takes on a whole new meaning. With limited resources but limitless determination, these individuals navigate the complexities of digitization, learning, adapting, and often succeeding against all odds.

This book, Digitizing Dreams, is a tribute to their indomitable spirit and the audacious journey of digitization. It chronicles the extraordinary stories of entrepreneurs who dared to dream beyond pen and paper, embracing technology not as an expense, but as a means to create profits and societal impact. It sheds light on their inspiring transition from traditional practices to modern solutions, capturing the essence of their grit and vision in a rapidly evolving world.

In a world of headlines dominated by unicorns and skyrocketing valuations, these stories bring a fresh perspective. While these small businesses may not be featured on magazine covers or celebrated in startup circles, they are the backbone of India's economy—driven by purpose, passion, and the relentless pursuit of betterment. They demonstrate that success isn't always about scale; sometimes, it's about the ripple effects of change, about the impact on one's family, employees, and community.

Beyond the numbers and technological advances, this is a story of hope, humanity, and the enduring power of dreams. Each chapter of this book delves into the lives of these digital warriors, revealing not only their entrepreneurial journeys but also their personal struggles, triumphs, and the profound impact of their efforts on society. It is a celebration of their courage, a reflection of their perseverance, and an inspiration for all who dare to dream.

Let us embark on this journey together, exploring the incredible tales of resilience, innovation, and transformation that define India's small business owners. Through their stories, we honor not just the power of technology but the spirit of the people who wield it to build a better future.

The Ghoshak journey of digitizing over 3,000 businesses has been nothing short of transformative—not just for our partners but for us as a team. Each business we've had the privilege to work with carries a unique essence, a distinct story shaped by its community, culture, and challenges. Yet, ten stories remain etched deeply in our memories. These aren't tales of sprawling metropolises with towering skyscrapers and buzzing corporate hubs. Instead, they are stories from the heartlands of India—small towns and cities where dreams are just as big, if not bigger.

These are places where the rhythm of life is intertwined with tradition, yet where innovation finds its place in the hands of bold entrepreneurs. Through these pages, you'll meet visionaries who measure success not in funding rounds or glittering awards but in the steady growth of profits and the joy reflected in their customers' smiles. Their journeys are a testament to the fact that the Indian digital dream is not confined to metro cities. It pulses with life and ambition across the villages, small towns, and bustling bazaars that form the soul of this country.

At Ghoshak, every team member plays the role of a digital warrior, not merely as enablers of technology but as partners in the journeys of these remarkable entrepreneurs. We walk alongside them, understanding their struggles, celebrating their victories, and finding innovative ways to help them scale, innovate, and achieve their dreams. It is an honor—a humbling privilege—to witness their transformations and to contribute to their success stories. Each small step forward feels monumental when you see the direct impact it has on their lives, their families, and their communities.

This book, however, is not just about businesses. It is about the spirit of entrepreneurship that refuses to bow to adversity. It is about the courage it takes to embrace change, to learn, unlearn, and evolve in a rapidly digitizing world. Above all, it is about the belief in technology as a great equalizer—a tool that bridges gaps, breaks barriers, and builds opportunities for those willing to harness its power.

We hope these stories inspire you, as they have inspired us, to believe in the power of dreams, the promise of digitization, and the profound impact that small businesses have on shaping our society. These stories remind us of the incredible potential that lies within every dream, waiting to be digitized and brought to life.

Let's celebrate the unsung heroes of India's digital revolution. Let their journeys remind us that behind every small business is a world of resilience, innovation, and hope—a world waiting to be acknowledged and empowered. Here's to the warriors, the dreamers, and the doers who dare to transform their visions into reality, creating ripples of change that reach far beyond their immediate surroundings.

With Warm Regards,
Digital Warrior

CHAPTER 1

Rooted Beginnings: The Urban Kirana Dream

In the early days of our journey at Ghoshak, every new lead was a beacon of hope and possibility. As a fledgling team fueled by ambition, we saw each connection as a thread weaving into the fabric of India's digital transformation. One afternoon, our inside sales team, always on the lookout for promising prospects, shared an intriguing lead that immediately caught our attention. It was from a small family in Chennai, a family that had recently moved from a Tier 2 city in Tamil Nadu. They were embarking on a venture to establish a kirana shop—a quintessential Indian grocery store.

What set this lead apart wasn't just their aspiration but their progressive outlook on integrating technology into a traditional business. The idea of marrying the old with the new, especially in an industry where most preferred the tried-and-tested methods, was refreshing and sparked our curiosity.

The family in question was a joint family, deeply rooted in their values and traditions. Like many Indian families, their lives revolved around shared meals, collective decision-making, and an enduring sense of togetherness. The matriarch, a dignified woman with a commanding presence, had made the pivotal decision to revive their age-old family business. However, what stood out was the shift in leadership—the daughter-in-law, a young and determined woman, was at the forefront of this initiative. Her vision was bold

Krishna

yet grounded: to breathe new life into the family's kirana shop using modern technology like point-of-sale (POS) systems and stock management software.

When we received the lead, we were both excited and intrigued. Most kirana shops, especially those just starting out, relied heavily on the pen-and-paper method for managing transactions and inventory. The idea that this modest 1,000-square-foot shop sought a technological upgrade was not just surprising

—it was revolutionary in its own right.

Determined to understand their aspirations better, we decided to meet them in person. Back then, we believed that face-to-face interactions were irreplaceable. There's something profoundly human about sitting across from someone, sharing stories, exchanging ideas, and building trust in a way that emails and phone calls can never replicate. So, we packed our demo equipment, brimming with excitement, and set off for the meeting.

As we arrived at their shop nestled in the bustling heart of the city, we were greeted with warmth and enthusiasm. The shopfront, though modest, was brimming with life. Customers weaved in and out, and the faint aroma of spices and grains filled the air. The family welcomed us with open arms, introducing each member with pride. The patriarch, a man of few words but with an undeniable aura of wisdom, observed us keenly. His son, the primary breadwinner, exuded a quiet confidence, while the daughter-in-law, the driving force behind this modern initiative, greeted us with an infectious energy.

The shop itself was a testament to their meticulous nature. Despite its compact size, every corner was thoughtfully organized. Shelves were neatly stacked with an array of products, from everyday essentials to local specialties. It was clear that the family took immense pride in their establishment, and their passion resonated in every detail.

After settling in, we began setting up our equipment for the demo. As the equipment was laid out, the shop slowly transformed into a small community gathering. The immediate family wasn't the only audience; neighbors and curious passersby joined in, drawn by the novelty of the event. The daughter- in-law stood front and center, her eyes gleaming with anticipation.

The demo session turned into an engaging and interactive experience. We walked them through the functionalities of our POS software, showcasing how it could simplify their billing process, streamline inventory management, and even provide insightful analytics to help them make data-driven decisions. Questions poured in, from the family and the onlookers alike, and we answered each one with enthusiasm, relishing the opportunity to connect with them on a deeper level.

What struck us most was the family's deliberation before making this decision. Their choice to embrace technology wasn't a spur-of-the-moment idea. The daughter-in-law, in particular, had spent months researching, learning about digital tools, and weighing the pros and cons. It was her conviction and persistence that had convinced the family that this leap of faith was worth taking.

Her vision was crystal clear—she wanted their kirana shop to be more than just a corner store. She wanted it to thrive amidst the competitive urban market, to set an example for others in their community, and to prove that tradition and technology could coexist harmoniously. She dreamed of a future where the shop would be a symbol of resilience and innovation, serving as a beacon of possibility for others who dared to dream.

The demo lasted for about an hour, during which we patiently addressed a range of queries and concerns. From operational challenges to technological adaptability, the family had plenty of questions, all of which reflected their thoughtful approach. What stood out most was the family's collective decision-making. Even though the investment in our software was modest by broader standards, it was still significant for a small family-run business.

They didn't make the decision hastily. Over the next two days, they deliberated carefully, ensuring that every family member had a say. During this time, they reached out to us frequently—not just for advice about our software, but also for guidance on complementary decisions, like selecting the right printer, installing CCTV cameras, and even tips on optimizing their store layout.

Their inclusive approach was refreshing and inspiring. They didn't treat us as mere vendors but as trusted partners in their journey toward modernization. This level of involvement gave us a deep insight into the dynamics of family businesses and taught us an invaluable lesson: while SaaS products can be marketed and scaled globally, the Indian MSME sector thrives on trust, relationships, and a personal touch.

Over the following days, we worked closely with the family to install and set up the software. Their eagerness to learn and adapt was contagious, with each family member playing an active role. The daughter-in-law, the true visionary behind this transformation, took charge of training the staff. She patiently explained the system to each team member, ensuring they were comfortable with the new processes. Her determination and forward-thinking attitude were a driving force, proving that the fusion of tradition and technology was not only possible but also practical.

This experience illuminated the unique dynamics of family-run businesses in India. Decisions weren't made by a single individual but were a collective endeavor. The patriarch's approval lent authority, the son's practical concerns grounded the discussion, and the daughter-in-law's vision provided direction. Each perspective was valued, culminating in a decision that reflected the entire family's aspirations

Reflecting on this experience, we realized why many SaaS startups struggle to sustain momentum in the MSME sector after initial successes. It's not just about offering a great product; it's about understanding the cultural nuances, going the extra mile to support clients, and building relationships that transcend the transactional. In a country like India, where trust often outweighs the tangible, the human element is indispensable.

When we finally left their shop after completing the setup, we felt a profound sense of accomplishment. This wasn't just about closing a sale; it was about being part of a family's transformation—helping them navigate the bridge between tradition and technology. This experience became a cornerstone for us at Ghoshak, shaping our customer-first philosophy and reaffirming our belief in the transformative power of personal connections.

"Rooted Beginnings: The Urban Kirana Dream" isn't merely a story about a small family venturing into a new chapter. It's a testament to the resilience and adaptability of Indian MSMEs. It's about the courage to embrace change, the harmony of blending old and new, and the undeniable fact that at the heart of every business are people—relationships and dreams waiting to be digitized.

Key Takeaway:

Technology adoption in traditional setups thrives on trust and relationships. Digitization is not just a technical upgrade but a cultural transformation led by collaboration.

CHAPTER 2

From Home to Homepage – Latha's Saree Success

In the bustling town of Coimbatore, renowned for its vibrant cultural heritage and thriving marketplaces, lay the home and showroom of Mrs. Latha, a passionate entrepreneur. Her small-scale saree business had been her pride and joy for years. Each saree in her collection was handpicked with care, a reflection of her dedication to preserving traditional craftsmanship. From intricately woven Kanchipuram silks to elegant Chanderis, her living room had been transformed into a treasure trove of beauty and artistry.

Despite her unwavering passion and a loyal local customer base, Latha found her business growth stagnant. Most of her sales came from friends, family, and neighbors who spread the word about her exquisite sarees. While this brought a steady income, she often felt frustrated by her inability to expand beyond her immediate circle.

One sunny afternoon, our team decided to visit her and explore how we could help. Upon entering her home, we were welcomed with warmth and genuine hospitality. As we admired her collection, she shared her journey, dreams, and the challenges she faced.

"It's not that people don't like my sarees," she explained over a steaming cup of chai. "It's just that I don't know how to reach more people. I've tried advertising locally, but it hasn't made much of a difference."

We listened carefully and identified the key issue: lack of discoverability. While her sarees were undoubtedly unique and high-quality, they were limited to a physical space. In today's digital age, this was a significant barrier to growth.

We suggested creating a website and an online store to showcase her sarees to a wider audience. At first, Latha was hesitant. "I'm not very tech-savvy," she admitted. "I wouldn't even know where to start."

Recognizing her apprehension, we proposed involving her daughter, Anu, a bright and tech-savvy high school student. Anu joined the conversation with an eager smile, and we shared our vision of how an online presence could elevate their business. Anu immediately grasped the potential and began persuading her mother.

"Amma, this could be a game-changer for us!" Anu exclaimed. "We can show your sarees to people all over India—maybe even the world! I'll help you every step of the way."

Her enthusiasm was infectious, and Latha finally agreed to give it a try. With Anu's support, we began the transformation.

First, we worked on creating a website that reflected Latha's love for sarees and her commitment to quality. The website was designed to be user-friendly and visually appealing, featuring high-resolution images of her collection. Each saree was accompanied by a detailed description highlighting its craftsmanship, material, and unique features.

To ensure a seamless shopping experience, we integrated a secure payment gateway and provided options for doorstep delivery. Additionally, we guided Latha and Anu on leveraging social media to promote their business. Platforms like Instagram and Facebook became their new storefronts, where they showcased their sarees and engaged with customers.

Initially, the transition was overwhelming for Latha. "This is all so new," she confessed during one of our training sessions. But her determination to succeed outweighed her fears. With Anu by her side, she learned how to update inventory, respond to customer inquiries, and even post promotional content online.

One of the most heartwarming moments was seeing Anu teach her mother how to take attractive photos of the sarees using natural light. "Amma, tilt the phone a little—yes, perfect! Look how beautiful this one looks now," she said, showing her mother the results.

As days turned into weeks, Latha grew more confident in managing her online store. Orders started coming in from places she'd never even heard of, and each new customer brought a renewed sense of excitement.

"I never thought I'd be able to sell my sarees outside Coimbatore," Latha said with a grateful smile during a follow-up visit. "Now, I feel like the whole country is my market."

Through this journey, Latha not only expanded her business but also grew as an entrepreneur. Her story became a testament to the power of blending tradition with technology, proving that with the right support and determination, even the most traditional businesses could thrive in the digital era.

Within the first three months of launching her website, Mrs. Latha's business experienced a remarkable 30% growth. Orders began pouring in from various corners of the country, not just from Coimbatore. The online store had opened doors to a diverse audience, giving people access to her exquisite sarees, many of whom had never heard of her before. The combination of convenience, a wide selection, and the unmatched quality of her products quickly made her business a hit in the digital space.

The positive feedback and influx of orders brought a newfound confidence to Mrs. Latha. She was thrilled to see her hard work and passion being recognized on such a broad scale. One day, we received an excited call from her.

"I've been thinking," she began, her voice brimming with enthusiasm, "if the saree business can flourish online, why not my homemade pickles and snacks? It's another thing I've always been passionate about. Can we create an online store for that too?"

Her request didn't surprise us—her confidence and entrepreneurial spirit had grown significantly since we first met her. Seeing the potential for another success story, we immediately agreed to help her replicate the process.

This experience wasn't just a milestone for Mrs. Latha; it was deeply fulfilling for our team as well. Watching her transition from a hesitant entrepreneur to a confident digital business owner reinforced our commitment to supporting small businesses. Her story reminded us of the importance of personalized support in helping traditional entrepreneurs adapt to modern challenges.

By identifying her pain points and tailoring solutions, we gained her trust and loyalty, creating a partnership built on mutual respect and shared goals

For Mrs. Latha, the journey was transformative. Not only did she expand her reach and revenue, but she also discovered a new sense of empowerment and a vision for the future. Her sarees and pickles weren't just products anymore— they were bridges connecting her heritage and craftsmanship to people far beyond her physical showroom.

Her success underscored a powerful truth: embracing digital transformation, coupled with dedicated guidance, can unlock limitless possibilities for traditional businesses.

As we continue to work with entrepreneurs like Mrs. Latha, her story remains a shining example of the resilience and potential within small businesses. It serves as a constant reminder of why we do what we do: to enable growth, foster innovation, and make a lasting impact in the lives of those we serve.

Key Takeaway:

Digitization amplifies discoverability. With the right tools and personalized support, even home-run businesses can evolve into thriving digital brands.

CHAPTER 3

The Mesh Revolution

When the father-and-son duo walked into our office, it was clear they shared a bond deeper than business. They weren't just partners—they were friends, two generations united by a shared vision. Their ambition? To launch India's first online platform for ordering mosquito mesh, revolutionizing how customers protect their homes from insects.

From the very first meeting, their openness and collaborative approach stood out. They didn't treat this as a mere business transaction; it felt like a joint mission. This shared commitment laid the foundation for a partnership that would become transformative—not just for their business, but for us at Ghoshak as well.

Our team quickly dove in, analyzing their existing processes and benchmarking against industry standards. We understood that achieving something groundbreaking required thorough preparation. Assuring the duo that we were invested in doing it right, we bought the time needed to craft a robust strategy.

By the time the second meeting came around, we presented a comprehensive plan. We envisioned a seamless digital journey for their customers—one that began with the first click and ended with satisfied reviews. The focus was on designing a user-friendly, world-class website that empowered customers to make informed choices about the mosquito mesh they needed.

Throughout the project, we kept them actively involved. During the third meeting, we delved into the backend design of the digital customer experience. The son, with his sharp vision and customer-centric mindset, inspired us with his dedication to ensuring that customers choose the right mesh for their needs. His passion pushed us to innovate beyond the ordinary.

In just 90 days—after numerous online meetings and countless brainstorming sessions over coffee and bajjis—their vision became a reality. The website was live, replicating the trust and confidence of an in-store experience. It was more than just a website; it was a digital leap forward.

But our journey didn't end there. Instead of simply delivering the project and moving on, we chose to stay by their side for the next six months. This decision proved pivotal, allowing us to refine and enhance their operations while learning alongside them.

One major insight we uncovered was the enduring importance of physical touchpoints in a digital world. While the website was an excellent enabler, customers purchasing technical products like mosquito mesh still valued seeing and feeling the product firsthand.

We suggested opening mini display centers across South India to complement the online platform. The father, ever accommodating, embraced the idea wholeheartedly. The result was extraordinary. Their conversion rate soared from 7% to 20%. Today, they have nine display centers and are on track to open 25 by mid-2025.

This journey wasn't just about digitizing their business; it was about achieving tangible growth. For us at Ghoshak, it reinforced the idea that true digital transformation is about enhancing the customer experience and driving real business success.

The process wasn't without its challenges. A misplaced order once had us scrambling to adjust the backend. Late-night calls from the son to discuss customer feedback became routine. And when they celebrated their first 100 online orders, we joined in, cheering like it was our own success.

These moments—some small, some monumental—added richness to our journey. They reminded us that every challenge, every breakthrough, and every celebration is part of a larger story.

Key Takeaway:

True digitization delivers measurable outcomes. A seamless blend of online and offline strategies can boost conversion rates while fostering trust.

CHAPTER 4

The Kulfi Chronicles

When the founders of an emerging kulfi brand walked into our office, it was clear this was going to be a unique journey. Unlike many clients who begin with uncertainty, they arrived with a crystal-clear vision: to establish a robust franchise model that would transform their brand into a household name. Their request was as ambitious as it was focused—they needed a website that would serve as the digital cornerstone for their franchise expansion.

What set them apart was their unwavering trust in us. "We're here to share our requirements," one of the founders said during our first meeting, "but we'll trust you to deliver." That level of confidence and autonomy set the tone for a truly collaborative and inspiring partnership.

Understanding the Vision

The first step was to immerse ourselves in their world and understand the nuances of the kulfi industry. This wasn't just about creating a visually stunning website; it was about building a platform that could embody the brand's ethos and appeal to aspiring franchisees.

Our team dove deep into research—analyzing market trends, studying the challenges faced by franchise businesses, and examining successful food and beverage franchise models. Through this process, we identified three key expectations from potential franchisees:

KULFI
KULFI ICE

1. Clarity about the brand's profitability and the support system provided to franchisees.
2. Efficiency in the onboarding process, ensuring an easy transition to becoming a franchise partner.
3. Trust in the brand's operational excellence, offering confidence that the partnership would be a success.

Armed with these insights, we set out to craft a website that would be more than just informative—it had to build excitement, trust, and a sense of opportunity.

The Foundation of Growth

Within a month, we launched the website—a vibrant, user-friendly platform tailored to meet the founders' goals. It featured interactive tools like:

ROI Calculator: Helping potential franchisees estimate their returns and understand the financial benefits of partnering with the brand.

Step-by-Step Onboarding Guides: Simplifying the journey from inquiry to ownership.

Success Stories: Highlighting the achievements of their initial franchisees, creating a sense of credibility and inspiration.

The website didn't just provide information; it became a virtual gateway to the kulfi revolution, designed to answer every question a prospective partner might have while capturing the brand's authentic and colorful essence.

Scaling Beyond Digital

As inquiries began flooding in, the founders realized that scaling their franchise network required more than a digital presence. They needed robust operational processes to handle the growth.

We stepped in once again, this time to develop a custom franchise management system. This system became the backbone of their operations, streamlining critical aspects such as:

Inventory Tracking: Ensuring each franchise had the right supplies at the right time.

Royalty Calculations: Automating complex financial processes for accuracy and efficiency.

Performance Dashboards: Giving the founders real-time insights into the health of their franchise network.

This comprehensive system didn't just support their rapid growth; it enabled it. By automating and simplifying operations, the brand was able to onboard new franchisees seamlessly, maintaining their standards of quality and efficiency as they expanded.

A Shared Success Story

Today, the kulfi brand stands as a shining example of what's possible with the right mix of vision, trust, and execution. Their franchise network continues to grow, bringing the rich flavors of their kulfi to homes across the country.

For us at Ghoshak, this journey was about more than delivering a project—it was about being part of a story that celebrated entrepreneurship, innovation, and the joy of creating something enduring.

A Journey of Collaboration

Over the next three years, our partnership with the kulfi brand grew stronger, evolving into a relationship marked by trust, creativity, and shared ambition. Together, we embarked on new initiatives that expanded their reach and strengthened their brand.

We launched targeted digital campaigns, carefully designed to attract franchisees in key cities and towns. Each campaign highlighted the unique opportunities and benefits of joining the kulfi franchise family. Additionally, we crafted custom promotional materials to support their franchise partners, ensuring consistent branding and messaging across all locations.

The website became a living, breathing entity, continuously updated to reflect the brand's evolving goals. From introducing seasonal flavors to showcasing franchise success stories, the site remained a hub of engagement and information.

Milestones of Success

The impact of these efforts was undeniable. By the end of the first year, the brand had signed agreements with 25 franchisees. By the end of the third year, they had surpassed 100 franchises across India—a monumental achievement that called for celebration.

Through every milestone, the collaborative dynamic between our teams remained seamless. The secret to this harmony? A foundation of mutual respect.

The founders trusted our expertise and processes, giving us the autonomy to execute their vision, while we respected their clarity and deep understanding of their business. As one of the founders succinctly put it:

"You know our requirements, and we understand your schedule and speed. That's why we have a sync."

Lessons in Partnership

This journey was more than a business engagement; it was a masterclass in building and nurturing client relationships.

The kulfi founders didn't just have a clear vision—they recognized the importance of aligning with our workflows. This mutual understanding turned potential roadblocks into stepping stones, making changes, campaigns, and iterations feel like part of a shared mission rather than a negotiation.

Challenges were inevitable, from adapting to market trends to scaling their digital infrastructure to meet growing demands. Yet, each obstacle was met with a collaborative spirit, making problem-solving not just effective but also rewarding.

Building a Legacy

Looking back, it's evident that this journey wasn't just about websites or campaigns. It was about shaping a dream into a tangible, thriving reality.

Their success isn't just reflected in numbers—100 franchises and counting— but in the way their brand has become synonymous with quality and trust in the kulfi industry.

For us, the most significant reward wasn't just the projects we completed but the trust they placed in us and the lessons we learned along the way. It reaffirmed our belief that the strongest partnerships are built on:

- Clarity of vision,
- Mutual trust, and
- A shared commitment to excellence.

A Testament to Digitization

As the kulfi brand continues to flourish, we remain proud to have played a part in their journey. This experience serves as a reminder that **digitization thrives when technology aligns seamlessly with**

a clear vision, mutual trust, and a commitment to achieving real business outcomes.

Their story, and ours, is a testament to the power of collaboration, proving that with the right foundation, even the sweetest dreams can grow into lasting legacies.

Key Takeaway:

Digitization flourishes with clarity and mutual respect. A well-aligned partnership, coupled with robust digital tools, can scale visionary ideas into sustainable success.

CHAPTER 5

The Delivery Dreamer

It was a routine afternoon when my team approached me with an unusual request. They had been in discussions with a young man from a Tier 2 city who had a bold dream of starting a hyperlocal delivery business in his hometown. The excitement in their voices was palpable, but I remained skeptical.

"A delivery business?" I raised an eyebrow. "Without deep pockets? Let's not waste our time."

But my team insisted, urging me to meet him, if only to hear his vision. Begrudgingly, I agreed, prepared to politely listen and move on to more promising opportunities.

Then he walked into the room.

In his early twenties, this young man carried an energy that was impossible to ignore. There was a spark in his eyes—a fire that burned with ambition. His passion was contagious, his ideas sharp and thoughtful, and his determination evident in every word he spoke.

Here was someone who didn't just have a vision—he had the grit and persistence to turn it into reality. For the first time in a long while, I was left speechless, my doubts slipping away one by one.

Without further hesitation, we agreed to take on his project. The challenge was simple yet profound: we had to build a cost-effective

DELIVERY

platform that could meet his high expectations, without requiring a massive investment.

90 Days of Action

What followed was three months of relentless effort. The young entrepreneur didn't just bring ideas to the table; he brought insights, raw energy, and a commitment that fueled our entire team. Together, we dived deep into understanding his hometown, analyzing everything from local customer needs to logistical challenges.

This wasn't just a project; it felt like a shared mission. He was with us every step of the way—giving feedback, suggesting tweaks, and ensuring we understood the cultural and economic nuances of his market. Together, we built a lean, efficient platform designed for success.

The day of the launch arrived, and the results were nothing short of extraordinary. From the very first order, it was clear this wasn't just another business—it was the start of something bigger. Within weeks, his daily orders skyrocketed from 10 to over 70. The success story quickly spread throughout his town, inspiring others to take a chance and pursue their own dreams.

Beyond His Own Dream

But this young man's vision didn't end with his own success. Instead of sitting back and enjoying his newfound achievements, he came back to our office, this time with two friends in tow, each from different cities. He was eager to share his formula, to help others replicate his success.

This selflessness struck a deep chord within me. Here was someone who could have easily focused solely on his own growth, yet he chose to uplift and empower others. In his eyes, success wasn't a solitary journey—it was about building a community and sharing the wealth of opportunity.

His friends went on to become entrepreneurs in their own right, each launching their own delivery businesses with our assistance. One after another, they began to succeed, their stories interwoven with the same ambition and determination that had driven the original entrepreneur.

A Ripple Effect

As I reflected on this journey, I couldn't help but admire the power of collaboration. It was clear that this wasn't just a business venture—it was a movement that had touched the lives of many. The ripple effect of one young man's determination had sparked a fire in others, each taking the leap to build something meaningful for themselves.

For us, the reward wasn't just seeing a platform come to life or scaling a business—it was witnessing the profound impact that one dream could have on an entire community. The young entrepreneur had created a legacy, not just for himself, but for others who believed they could achieve greatness as well.

The lessons were clear: success isn't just about having a vision. It's about perseverance, community, and most importantly, the willingness to share that success with others.

The Birth of Gho Delivery

The success of that young man inspired us to think much bigger. Why limit ourselves to just one town or a handful of entrepreneurs? Why not create something that could empower many more dreamers? With that in mind, we set out to create something larger—a platform dedicated to hyperlocal delivery businesses. And so, Gho Delivery was born.

Today, Gho Delivery stands as a thriving product that supports over 50 entrepreneurs across various cities. These individuals are not just running businesses—they're creating jobs, serving their communities, and proving that with the right tools and unwavering determination, success is within reach.

Our commitment to making the product accessible to all meant we deliberately kept it cost-effective, ensuring that anyone, regardless of their financial background, could take their first step into the world of entrepreneurship.

Lessons in Humility

This journey has been a humbling one, reminding me time and again that passion, persistence, and a strong sense of commitment can often surpass the power of deep pockets. I've seen firsthand how one person's success can spark a chain reaction, inspiring many others to take risks, build dreams, and achieve what they thought was impossible.

What stood out to me most was the realization that this was not just about business—it was about empowering others to create their own legacies. The true essence of what we do at Ghoshak became clearer with every new entrepreneur who took their first step. This wasn't just about launching a product—it was about giving others the tools to turn their visions into reality.

A New Era Begins

Looking back, I understand now that this wasn't just another chapter in our journey—it was the beginning of a new era. The story of Gho Delivery wasn't written in spreadsheets or sales figures—it was written in the lives of the entrepreneurs we helped, each building their future with resilience and hope.

It all started with a single young dreamer who walked into our office, carrying nothing but his passion and an unwavering belief that he could make a difference. That moment sparked a fire that continues to burn brightly, shaping the future of Gho Delivery and all those it touches.

Key Takeaway:

True digitization is more than just technology; it's about empowering individuals to dream bigger, build better, and inspire others to do the same. When we build tools that unlock the potential of others, we don't just create businesses—we create movements.

CHAPTER 6

The Scent of Success

When the father and son duo behind Aromah walked into our office, the air itself seemed to carry the subtle elegance of their craft. Aromah wasn't just another business; it was a legacy—a family-run enterprise dedicated to the delicate art of fragrance-making. Their flagship store, nestled in the heart of Chennai, had been delighting customers for years with handcrafted blends that turned every visit into an experience—a sensory masterpiece.

Now, standing at the crossroads of tradition and innovation, they were ready to take a bold leap forward. Their vision was clear and twofold: launch an online store to bring their fragrances to a wider audience and build a robust system for seamless franchise expansion across South India.

What made this project even more intriguing was the dynamic between the father and son. The father, a seasoned expert in the intricate art of fragrance- making, had built his reputation around offering an exceptional, personalized customer experience. The son, on the other hand, was the embodiment of the next generation—ambitious, tech-savvy, and laser-focused on scaling the business rapidly. Together, they represented a fascinating blend of old-world charm and new-age ambition.

The Online Store: A Digital Extension of Elegance

Our journey began with building the online store, an essential step to achieving their vision. The father's primary concern was replicating

47

the personalized, high-touch experience their physical store was known for. "When someone walks into our store, they don't just buy a product—they buy a memory," he explained. Capturing that sense of intimacy and sensory experience in a digital format was no small task.

The son, however, had a different priority. "We need a system that's scalable," he said with quiet determination. "This isn't just about today's sales; it's about preparing for tomorrow's growth." His focus was on creating a platform that could not only serve the current customer base but also grow with the business as it expanded across South India.

The task was clear: create a platform that could strike a balance between the father's emphasis on personalization and the son's focus on scalability.

Building the Platform: Fusing Tradition with Technology

Over the course of weeks, we worked tirelessly with the Aromah team. Late- night brainstorming sessions became a staple, as we discussed everything from the finer points of user experience design to how we could marry high-tech solutions with the family's old-world ethos. The goal was to build something that felt as luxurious and personal as Aromah's physical store while still being efficient and scalable for the future.

Together, we created custom features like personalized fragrance recommendations, a guided shopping experience, and an elegant yet seamless checkout process. The goal was simple yet profound: to reflect the uniqueness of Aromah's brand in every digital interaction.

Launch Day: A New Chapter Begins

Launch day arrived, and with it came a mixture of nerves and excitement. We watched closely as the first orders began rolling in. From the way the platform handled customer interactions to the way it smoothly handled transactions, we knew we had succeeded in translating the essence of Aromah into the digital realm.

The result was beyond what we had imagined. Customers loved the convenience of shopping online without losing the bespoke feel of the brand. They could still enjoy the personal touch of the Aromah experience, from personalized fragrance suggestions to the thoughtful design that made the online store feel almost as intimate as the store in Chennai.

Expansion: Beyond the Online Store

With the online platform up and running, the next challenge was preparing for the franchise expansion. The son was eager to move quickly, while the father wanted to ensure that the same level of customer care and personal touch would be maintained at every new franchise location. This dynamic pushed us to think even further about what made Aromah special and how to preserve that in the franchise model.

The solution lay in creating a comprehensive, user-friendly system for franchisees to follow—from managing inventory to delivering an experience consistent with the brand's identity. With our digital platform in place, the foundation was set for a smooth and scalable franchise model.

The Scent of Success

The journey with Aromah was a perfect example of how tradition and innovation can work hand-in-hand. By merging the father's dedication to craftsmanship with the son's forward-thinking vision, we were able to create a digital presence that captured the essence of the brand while laying the groundwork for future growth.

Looking back, what made this project so special was the family dynamic. The father and son worked together with a mutual respect for each other's perspectives—one rooted in tradition, the other in progress. Their vision for the brand became clearer with each step we took, and it was an honor to be a part of that journey.

Through our partnership with Aromah, we learned that success isn't just about achieving business goals—it's about preserving what makes a brand unique while adapting to the needs of the future. And as Aromah continues to grow, we're proud to have helped create a platform that allows their fragrances to touch more lives, one scent at a time.

Franchise Expansion: The Art of Scaling Fragrances

With the online store running smoothly, it was time to tackle Aromah's second ambitious goal: franchise expansion. This phase presented a new set of challenges. Fragrance-making is far more than a business—it's an art. Every product, every fragrance, required a precise blend of raw materials, each with its own nuances. Ensuring that the same quality and experience could be replicated across multiple locations was no easy feat.

Our team dove deep into their operations, immersing ourselves in every aspect—from raw material procurement to SKU management. We didn't just want to replicate their existing processes; we wanted to enhance and scale them, ensuring that every franchise location could operate with the same level of care and craftsmanship that defined the flagship store.

Building a Scalable System

The result was a sophisticated franchise management system designed with scalability in mind. We carefully engineered processes that ensured operational efficiency without sacrificing the essence of the Aromah experience. From inventory tracking to training modules for franchisees, every detail was meticulously planned and executed.

Our goal was to make sure that every franchise, whether in a small town or a bustling city, could manage inventory seamlessly, provide consistent customer experiences, and uphold the quality that Aromah had become known for. The system included step-by-step training for new franchisees, a comprehensive approach to sourcing raw materials, and a robust inventory management platform

Building Bonds Beyond Business

As we navigated this journey together, something extraordinary happened. The countless meetings, discussions, and problem-solving sessions didn't just refine the business—they forged a personal bond between us. This wasn't just another project; it became a shared mission.

The father, with his deep wisdom, would often share stories about the early days of Aromah—how he built the business from the ground up, fueled by passion and dedication. The son, always forward-thinking, would speak passionately about his vision for the future—how technology could help Aromah reach new heights while preserving its soul. These moments were a reminder of why we do what we do: it wasn't just about creating platforms or systems; it was about becoming part of their story.

The Journey Continues: Aromah Today

Today, Aromah stands as a thriving business. Their flagship store in Chennai continues to captivate customers with its unique fragrances, while their growing network of franchises is expanding rapidly across South India. What began as a single-store operation has now transformed into a brand that's redefining how fragrances are experienced and distributed.

The journey hasn't been easy, but it has been deeply rewarding. With a blend of tradition and innovation, Aromah is flourishing—preserving the legacy of fragrance-making while embracing the opportunities of the digital age. The business is evolving, but its core values remain the same: a commitment to quality, a passion for craftsmanship, and a dedication to providing an unforgettable customer experience.

Lessons Learned

This project imparted invaluable lessons about working with multigenerational clients. The father's deep-rooted wisdom and the son's ambitious drive often pulled the team in different directions, creating a dynamic tension that pushed us to deliver our best work. This tension wasn't a hindrance—it was a catalyst, driving us to find creative solutions that respected the legacy of Aromah while enabling its growth.

It also reinforced the importance of balance—honouring tradition while embracing innovation. Aromah's journey taught us that when done right, the fusion of these elements can lead to something extraordinary.

Key Takeaway:

Digitization becomes truly transformative when it bridges the gap between generations, blending legacy with innovation to build a future-ready business.

CHAPTER 7

A Dream Sprouts and Grows: The Journey of Fresh Delivery

Ramesh's mornings stood in stark contrast to the hustle and bustle of the other residents in his apartment complex. While his neighbors scrambled to meet the demands of their corporate jobs, Ramesh found a quiet sense of fulfillment in delivering baskets of fresh, organic vegetables to the people living nearby. What began as a small, almost personal service—something he did in his spare time—soon grew into something far bigger than he had ever imagined.

He would buy fresh produce from local farmers and personally deliver it to the doorsteps of his neighbors, wrapping each item with the kind of care and attention to detail that spoke to his passion for fresh food and community. The joy he felt from these interactions was palpable, and over time, it became clear that his small act of kindness was something that could grow. What he had initially seen as a hobby was beginning to hint at something with far more potential.

Priya, his wife, had always supported Ramesh's passion. A dedicated IT professional, she worked long hours in the city but would often come home to find Ramesh busy delivering baskets and chatting with neighbors about the benefits of organic farming and fresh produce. While she admired his commitment, Priya also began to see something more: this hobby had the makings of a real business.

It wasn't just about delivering vegetables; it was about a community-driven movement that could help people live healthier lives.

One evening, after dinner, Priya casually asked, "What if we could grow this beyond just our building? What if we could bring fresh vegetables to more people, in more places?" The question struck a chord with Ramesh. It was more than just an idea—it was the spark they needed to see the bigger picture. They started talking about how they could scale this into a business, and Priya's IT expertise opened up a world of possibilities. With her experience in technology, she could see how they could streamline operations, manage inventory, and reach more customers.

But there was a significant challenge: as eager as they were to expand, the operation was still being run over WhatsApp. Orders were coming in from all directions, from neighbors to nearby localities, and Ramesh's personal touch— something he had built the business on—was beginning to suffer. With more and more people relying on them for fresh, organic vegetables, they knew they needed something more sophisticated, something that could manage their growing operations while still keeping the heart of the business intact.

That's when Priya and Ramesh reached out to us. Their request was simple but urgent: they needed a system that could manage hyper-local deliveries, track inventory, and keep them connected with their customers. But there was one major catch—they had a very tight budget. Most of the capital they had invested in the business came from personal savings and loans, so every penny counted.

The first meeting was eye-opening. As we sat down with them, we could feel their passion radiating from every word. Priya, with her background in IT, had already compiled a list of requirements that was both comprehensive and detailed. From tracking orders by apartment block numbers to ensuring timely weekly deliveries, her vision was clear. She even wanted features like automated reminders for customers to refill their baskets and the ability to customize orders based on dietary preferences. It was a vision that was ambitious but grounded in a deep understanding of the needs of the business.

The more we listened, the more we realized how specific their needs were. The challenge ahead seemed daunting—a system that could handle hyper-local deliveries, real-time updates, and constant monitoring. But despite the complexity, there was something undeniable about their determination. This wasn't just about building a business; it was about creating a community. Their goal wasn't to simply deliver vegetables; it was to build trust, nurture relationships, and positively impact the local economy by sourcing directly from farmers.

Our team was immediately drawn to their vision. This wasn't just another business to us; it felt like a calling. Ramesh and Priya weren't interested in running a generic delivery service. They wanted to create something that felt personal—something that touched people's lives in a meaningful way. And that was a mission we could get behind.

With this new understanding, we set out to build a solution that would allow Ramesh and Priya to manage their business efficiently while keeping that personal touch intact. We worked tirelessly to create a system that could scale their dream without sacrificing what made FreshDelivery unique. From a streamlined ordering platform to real-time inventory tracking, we made sure every aspect of their vision was accounted for.

As FreshDelivery grew, so did the sense of community. What had once been a small hobby had now blossomed into a business that was making a difference in the lives of so many. Ramesh and Priya's dream was taking shape—one basket at a time.

We knew this would take time and effort, but we were ready to work alongside Ramesh and Priya, helping bring their vision to life.

The journey wasn't without its struggles. Every new feature, every integration, required careful consideration and collaboration. Priya and Ramesh were deeply involved, offering their ideas and feedback, asking tough questions, and pushing us to do better. They had a clear vision, but their perfectionism sometimes slowed the process down. We spent countless hours brainstorming solutions, working out the logistics for the delivery system, refining the user interface, and figuring out how to keep every order fresh. Many late-night calls, endless cups of coffee, and back-and-forth discussions filled the weeks as we worked to get the system just right.

But despite the challenges, there was something that kept us pushing forward: their unwavering commitment. Ramesh and Priya weren't just building a business—they were building relationships with every one of their customers. They were determined to ensure that each basket of vegetables was perfect, each delivery arrived on time, and that their customers felt truly valued. Their insistence on sourcing only the best produce, directly from farmers who shared their values, set them apart. The care they took in packing and delivering each order was nothing short of inspiring. Each vegetable was wrapped carefully, each order was treated with love.

It wasn't just about the technology—it was about the experience. Priya and Ramesh ensured that every touchpoint in their service was crafted with care. They knew their customers by name, remembered their preferences, and worked tirelessly to ensure every delivery was seamless.

The project took longer than we had initially anticipated. There were plenty of roadblocks along the way, but it was all worth it. Today,

FreshConnect delivers over 1,000 orders a month. Ramesh and Priya, once dividing their time between India and the US, now manage the business remotely. They oversee everything—from inventory tracking and order processing to customer service—all thanks to the system we built together. What began as a hobby has blossomed into a thriving business, and they've managed to scale it while preserving the personal touch that made it special from the beginning.

Looking back, I'm reminded of something essential: small businesses can scale successfully when the founders have the right passion, clarity, and intent. Ramesh and Priya weren't just focused on making a profit—they wanted to make a difference. Their commitment to freshness, quality, and community was the heart of their success, and that made all the difference.

Key Takeaway:

Scaling a small business with digitization requires a perfect mix of passion, clarity, and the right systems to maintain the personal touch while expanding reach.

CHAPTER 8

The Aluminium Alchemist

Every industry has its moment of transformation, that pivotal point where it embraces change and sets itself on a path to innovation and growth. For us at Ghoshak, that moment came when we met Mr. Rajesh Kumar (name changed), a dynamic and ambitious entrepreneur in the aluminium windows industry. He wasn't just another manufacturer—he was a visionary with years of international experience and a relentless passion for his craft.

Rajesh had recently relocated to Tamil Nadu, determined to establish his brand across the state and eventually all of South India. The timing was critical: the aluminium windows sector, long dominated by unorganized players, was on the verge of getting structured. It was a chaotic yet opportunistic time, and Rajesh wanted to ensure that his brand didn't just survive the transition but flourished in it. The industry was ready for a transformation, and Rajesh was ready to lead it.

His challenge was clear: his customer and dealer onboarding process needed to be efficient, scalable, and appealing. Rajesh believed his products were a cut above the rest—sleek, durable, and designed to perfection. But his biggest concern was how to ensure these attributes resonated with potential dealers and customers without overwhelming them. He wanted a smooth, intuitive experience that would highlight the premium nature of his products while building a strong, recognizable brand that would leave a lasting impression.

When Rajesh approached us, we immediately knew this wouldn't be a standard, run-of-the-mill project. His expectations were high, and his passion for his products was palpable. He wasn't looking for just another vendor; he wanted a partner who shared his vision and could execute it with precision. Rajesh's commitment to quality was clear from the moment we began discussions. He had a clear sense of the direction he wanted his brand to take, and he was determined to get there—no matter how challenging the journey.

Crafting Simplicity in Complexity

The first challenge we tackled was simplifying the onboarding process. Aluminium windows might sound like an ordinary product to an outsider, but for Rajesh's business, every dealer or customer was an integral part of his growth engine. We designed a user-friendly digital platform that made the onboarding process not just easy but also engaging. We worked hard to strip away unnecessary complexity, ensuring that every step of the process felt natural and effortless. We wanted the platform to reflect the professionalism of Rajesh's brand—sleek, efficient, and built to last.

Rajesh's hands-on approach played a pivotal role in this. He was relentlessly involved throughout the process, offering feedback, sharing insights from his years of experience, and pushing us to elevate the project to the next level. His involvement wasn't just about guiding the project—it was about collaborating in real-time, constantly refining and improving every aspect. His vision was unwavering, and it fueled our team to deliver on his high expectations.

Beyond Digitization: The Campaign Revolution

As the project progressed, Rajesh made a bold request: Could we take over his brand's outreach campaigns? This wasn't part of our initial agreement, but we were excited about the opportunity. It gave us a chance to dive deeper into understanding his potential customers and partners. We knew we could bring fresh ideas to the table, so we agreed without hesitation.

The campaigns we developed together weren't just promotional—they were educational. Rajesh believed in the power of awareness, and he wanted to educate his customers about the advantages of choosing organized, high- quality aluminium window solutions over the traditional, unbranded options that flooded the market. The campaigns aimed to position Rajesh's brand as a trusted name in the industry, focusing on the long-term benefits of working with a professional, transparent, and innovative brand.

The results were nothing short of remarkable. As the campaigns took shape, dealers who had once been hesitant began to reach out in droves. Orders started to flow in at an impressive rate, and the recognition of Rajesh's brand grew exponentially. What had once been a small, niche venture was now a prominent player in the market. Dealers who had never considered selling high-quality, organized products now found themselves eager to partner with Rajesh. They saw the value not only in his products but in the whole experience that came with them—from the professional onboarding process to the educational outreach and the seamless customer service.

Rajesh's efforts weren't just about building a business—they were about transforming an entire industry. His willingness to invest in education, customer relationships, and branding set him apart from the countless other manufacturers in the market. He didn't want to just sell windows—he wanted to reshape the way people thought about the industry, and with each new dealer onboarded and each new customer served, he was doing just that.

Through every challenge and every triumph, Rajesh remained focused on his long-term vision. His passion for his craft, his commitment to quality, and his dedication to his customers were the driving forces behind his success. And as his brand continued to grow, it became clear that Rajesh's influence was far- reaching. What started as a small project—focused on streamlining onboarding and launching a brand—had evolved into a full-fledged campaign to revolutionize an entire industry.

Looking back, we realized that Rajesh had taught us something invaluable: true success comes not from just embracing technology, but from understanding the heart of the business and using technology to amplify its core values. His brand wasn't just about selling windows—it was about creating a legacy of quality, trust, and innovation that would stand the test of time.

Digitizing Quality Control

As our relationship with Rajesh continued to evolve, he entrusted us with another critical aspect of his business—quality control. In the aluminium window industry, quality is paramount, and customers often faced issues like misaligned frames, faulty locks, or improper seals. These problems could delay installations and cause significant dissatisfaction. For Rajesh, this wasn't just a logistical issue; it was a potential threat to his growing reputation. Customers demanded warranties and quick resolutions, and any delay in meeting these expectations could harm the trust he had worked so hard to build.

We understood the urgency of streamlining this process and ensuring that quality control was handled efficiently, without sacrificing accuracy. So, we digitized the quality control workflow. By moving the entire process online, we enabled Rajesh's team to issue warranties faster and more accurately, tracking each product from manufacturing to final inspection. The digital system provided instant access to quality checks, allowing Rajesh's team to identify issues and resolve them before they reached the customer.

This swift action improved overall customer satisfaction, and in turn, boosted loyalty and brand trust. It wasn't just about fixing problems—it was about preventing them and ensuring that every product that left the factory was a true representation of the brand's commitment to excellence.

A Website That Worked Wonders

For Rajesh, the website wasn't just another digital storefront—it was the very first impression his brand made to the outside world. His business wasn't merely about selling aluminium windows; it was about showcasing a level of professionalism, trustworthiness, and expertise that set his products apart from the competition. Knowing the importance of making a lasting first impression, we worked tirelessly to design a website that was not only visually appealing but also optimized for performance and searchability.

The website was sleek and user-friendly, a reflection of Rajesh's brand—sleek, modern, and practical. We optimized it with Search with Objectives (SWO), ensuring it would rank highly in search results and attract the right audience. Each page was designed to tell a story, from showcasing the product's features to educating potential customers on why they should choose Rajesh's brand over competitors. The clicks that came through weren't just numbers—they were genuine inquiries from dealers, contractors, and homeowners who were ready to make purchasing decisions. The website became a key tool in converting interest into tangible business opportunities, driving sales and building the brand's online presence.

The AI Edge: Smart Scoring for Partners

Perhaps our most significant contribution to Rajesh's expansion strategy was the development of an AI-powered smart scoring platform to assist in onboarding new partners. This innovative tool assessed potential dealers based on key criteria, such as market reach, sales potential, and creditworthiness, ensuring that Rajesh only partnered with the most qualified businesses. Instead of relying on subjective judgment or time-consuming manual checks,

the AI platform provided a data-driven approach to evaluating potential dealers, streamlining the process, and making it faster, more accurate, and more efficient.

The AI system analyzed a variety of factors, from financial stability to regional demand, helping Rajesh identify and select partners who were not only capable of meeting the demands of his business but were also aligned with his vision for growth. This process saved Rajesh time, minimized risks, and gave him the confidence to scale his operations, knowing that he was partnering with companies that would uphold the standards of his brand. The smart scoring platform was a game-changer, allowing Rajesh to build a network of reliable, high-performing dealers that could support his ambitious plans for expansion.

Lessons from Aluminium

This project taught us one critical lesson that would resonate in all of our future endeavors: some businesses require the right mix of offline and online strategies to truly scale and succeed. In Rajesh's case, while digital tools brought efficiency, scale, and a streamlined approach to processes like quality control, partner onboarding, and marketing, his personal touch was irreplaceable. His presence in the field, his face-to-face meetings with dealers, and his dedication to building relationships with customers played an equally crucial role in building trust.

We saw how digital strategies and human connection could coexist in a powerful synergy. While we provided the technology to simplify processes, Rajesh's genuine passion for his work and his personal involvement in the day- to-day operations of his business created a bond that no algorithm could replace. His hands-on approach to ensuring that every dealer was fully supported, and that every customer's needs were met, ensured the brand's success.

By the end of our journey together, Rajesh's brand was no longer just another player in the aluminium windows industry—it was a rising star, leading the transition toward a more organized, professional sector. His brand's name became synonymous with quality, innovation, and trust, and it was clear that he had found the perfect balance between leveraging technology and maintaining personal relationships. For us, it was a powerful reminder that digitization isn't just about adopting the latest technologies—it's about understanding how to use these tools to reimagine processes, simplify operations, and make the business more impactful.

Key Takeaway:

Digitization isn't just about technology; it's about reimagining processes, making them simpler, scalable, and impactful, even in traditionally unorganized industries.

CHAPTER 9

Sweet Dreams Turned Digital

When we first met the visionary behind Tamil Nadu's iconic palkova brand, we knew this was no ordinary entrepreneur. With a legacy dating back to 1988, he had built his reputation on crafting the finest palkova—a South Indian delicacy cherished for its rich, creamy texture and authentic taste. His story was the stuff of legends, a tale of perseverance and vision. Over the decades, he had single-handedly transformed palkova from a humble sweet into a household name, not by opening his own chain of shops but by supplying his signature delicacy to sweet shops and bakeries across the state.

This wasn't just a business for him—it was a movement, a revolution that had taken him across Tamil Nadu, building relationships, earning trust, and spreading the taste of his palkova far and wide. Now, he had a new dream: to make his brand a Direct-toConsumer (D2C) powerhouse, bringing palkova directly to homes across South India while seamlessly integrating his existing B2B and B2B2C operations.

When he approached us at Ghoshak with his vision, we were both inspired and humbled. Here was a man who had spent decades perfecting his craft and mastering the nuances of offline business, now seeking to embrace the world of digital commerce with the same passion and dedication.

A Visionary with a Hands-On Approach:

From our very first meeting, it was evident that this wasn't going to be a typical client relationship. He didn't just delegate tasks—

he immersed himself in every detail. His understanding of the customer journey, honed over decades of offline interactions, was unparalleled. He shared insights about customer preferences, buying patterns, and even the emotional connection people had with palkova.

For him, the online store wasn't just about selling a product—it was about replicating the rich, sensory experience of buying palkova in person. "When someone buys palkova, they're not just buying a sweet. They're buying nostalgia, trust, and tradition, " he told us. It became our mission to translate that essence into a digital experience.

Today, the brand stands as a shining example of omni-channel success. Whether it's a customer ordering a single box of palkova online, a sweet shop stocking up for festival season, or a bakery adding the product to its menu, the experience is seamless and satisfying.

Lessons in Humility and Adaptability:

This journey wasn't just about building a platform—it was about learning from a master. His willingness to embrace change, his attention to detail, and his unwavering commitment to his customers taught us valuable lessons about what it means to be a true entrepreneur.

What struck us most was his humility. Despite his success, he remained grounded, always eager to learn and improve. It was this attitude that made the project not just successful, but deeply rewarding.

Key Takeaway:

Blending offline insights with online innovation enables legacy businesses to maintain authenticity while building future-ready omni-channel operations.

CHAPTER 10

Revolutionizing Electronics

When the entrepreneur first walked into our office, his energy was infectious. He wasn't the kind to sit back and wait for things to happen—he was a doer, someone who had carved his way from humble beginnings with sheer determination and a hunger to serve his customers better. From running a small electronics shop in a Tier 3 city to envisioning a platform that could take on the e-commerce giants, his journey was a testament to grit and ambition.

But when he told us his dream, we were skeptical. The electronics space was dominated by well-funded juggernauts, with cutthroat competition, wafer-thin margins, and relentless price wars. "Are you sure you want to do this?" we asked, candidly outlining the challenges.

His response silenced the room. "You're reading magazines and business newspapers and giving me gyan, " he said, a mix of frustration and confidence in his tone. "I'm on the ground. I talk to my customers every day. I know the gaps in the market. Electronics isn't just about low prices—it's about personal touch, great service, and trust. If we can deliver those, we'll win. Support me, and I promise you, we'll make it happen."

It wasn't just his conviction that won us over—it was his deep understanding of the market. This wasn't someone diving in without preparation. He had already built a service network across the state, offering reliable after-sales support that most big players lacked.

He was sourcing high-quality, affordable products from across the globe, ensuring his customers got the best value. He had done the groundwork; all he needed was a platform to amplify his reach.

A Simple Yet Powerful Vision His clarity of vision was remarkable. He didn't want a flashy website or unnecessary bells and whistles. "I want something simple, effective, and customer-friendly, " he said. "The focus should be on trust—clear product information, transparent pricing, and seamless service."

Our team got to work, building an e-commerce platform that mirrored his philosophy. The interface was straightforward yet elegant, with easy navigation and detailed product descriptions. We integrated tools to highlight his USP—service guarantees and customer support availability. The platform also included dynamic pricing features, allowing him to respond quickly to market trends.

While we worked on the tech, he worked tirelessly on the backend. He built relationships with suppliers, fine-tuned his logistics, and strengthened his service network. His attention to detail was inspiring—every decision, no matter how small, was driven by his commitment to his customers.

From 1 Store to Serving the Masses:

The platform launched, and the results were beyond what any of us had anticipated. In the first month alone, he achieved sales volumes that rivaled established players in his region. Customers loved the combination of affordable products, reliable service, and the ease of shopping online.

As word spread, his business grew exponentially. Today, he is achieving an impressive Monthly Recurring Revenue (MRR) of ₹50 lakh, selling products with a maximum MRP of ₹4,000. His service network, which spans the entire state, ensures that every customer feels supported—a critical differentiator in a market often plagued by poor after-sales experiences.

What's most remarkable is that his growth hasn't been fueled by deep pockets or flashy marketing. It's been powered by his deep understanding of customer needs, his willingness to adapt, and his relentless work ethic.

Lessons in Humility and Determination:

For us, this project was more than just another assignment. It was a humbling reminder of the power of vision and perseverance. Here was a man who didn't let market realities or competition intimidate him. Instead, he saw them as challenges to overcome.

A Platform for the Deserving:

Reflecting on his story, we feel blessed to have played a small role in his success. Digital technology is a great equalizer, opening doors for entrepreneurs who might not have the resources to compete traditionally but have the drive to succeed.

For him, the journey is just beginning. His vision is to expand beyond his state, reaching customers across the country and perhaps even internationally. And with his passion and customer-first approach, we have no doubt he'll get there.

Key Takeaway:

When ground-level insights meet the right digital platform, even resource-constrained entrepreneurs can challenge industry giants and redefine customer experiences.

The D.E.A.R. Framework: Empowering MSMEs to Go Digital

After working with over 3,000 startups and MSMEs through Ghoshak, a key insight became clear: the two biggest challenges faced by MSMEs in scaling their businesses are discoverability and managing enquiries effectively. Despite having great products and services, many small businesses struggle to be found by their target customers, and even when they do, they often lack the tools to convert enquiries into sales.

This led me to design the D.E.A.R. Framework—a simple, actionable model to help MSMEs digitize their business processes and tackle these challenges head-on. The framework focuses on the four critical pillars of growth: Discovery, Engagement, Acquisition, and Retention.

- Discovery: Helps businesses establish an online presence to ensure they are visible to their target audience, leveraging tools like Google My Business, social media, and location-based ads.
- Engagement: Guides MSMEs in effectively connecting with potential customers through chatbots, WhatsApp Business, and valuable content.
- Acquisition: Focuses on converting leads into customers through lead management systems, instant quotation tools, and fostering trust via reviews.
- Retention: Encourages businesses to nurture relationships with customers using automated follow-ups, feedback collection, and loyalty programs.

The D.E.A.R. Framework is grounded in practical experience from real-world challenges faced by MSMEs I've worked with. It breaks down the complex journey of digitization into manageable steps, making it easier for small businesses to grow and thrive in a digital-first world. This framework has already helped several businesses improve their lead generation and enquiry management, and I hope it serves as a guiding light for many more.

By adopting the D.E.A.R. Framework, MSMEs can position themselves for sustainable growth, increased discoverability, and a more structured approach to handling enquiries—a vital step toward digitizing their dreams.

D.E.A.R. Framework (Discovery, Engage, Acquire, Retain)

1. **Discovery**

   Online Presence Setup: Create a Google My Business profile and list on relevant platforms (Justdial, IndiaMART, etc.).

   Website and SEO: Build a simple website with optimized keywords related to your business for search visibility.

   Social Media: Use platforms like Instagram, Facebook, and LinkedIn for visibility based on your target audience.

   Location-Based Ads: Run geo-targeted ads on Google and Facebook to attract local customers.

2. **Engage**

   Chat Tools: Integrate chatbots or live chat on your website for real-time customer interactions.

   WhatsApp Business: Use it for quick responses to enquiries and sharing product/service catalogs.

   Content Marketing: Share blogs, videos, or testimonials to educate and engage potential customers.

3. **Acquire**

   Lead Management: Use a CRM tool to track and manage leads effectively. **Instant Quotation Tools:** Provide easy options for customers to request quotes or information online.

   Online Reviews: Encourage happy customers to leave positive reviews on Google and other platforms for credibility.

4. **Retain**

Follow-Up Automation: Use tools like email marketing or WhatsApp campaigns to follow up on enquiries.
Feedback and Improvement: Collect customer feedback digitally (via forms or surveys) to improve services.
Loyalty Programs: Introduce reward systems to keep repeat customers engaged.

A Way Forward

As we Continue Digitalizing Entrepreneur's Dreams, I hope you're inspired by the incredible potential of digital transformation in the MSME landscape. This book isn't just a collection of case studies and insights—it's a call to action for every small business owner, entrepreneur, and dreamer to embrace the tools and technologies that can redefine their future.

Digitization is not merely about adopting new tools; it's about a shift in mindset—a willingness to evolve, innovate and envision a future that transcends traditional boundaries. The story shared in this book proves that even the smallest enterprises can achieve extraordinary growth with the right strategies, commitment, and adaptability.

At Ghoshak, we've witnessed firsthand the challenges and triumphs of businesses navigating this journey. While the road to transformation is often fraught with uncertainties, the rewards are unparalleled: efficiency, scalability, resilience, and, most importantly, the empowerment to dream bigger than ever before.

In a rapidly changing world, it's crucial that we equip our MSME Entrepreneur's not just to survive but to thrive and compete with MNC. With the power of digitization, we can pave the way for a more inclusive, innovative, and prosperous economy.

To every reader: the time to act is now. Let your journey toward digitization be the bridge to fulfilling your dreams, and may your story one day inspire others to take the leap.

Thank you for embarking on this journey with us. Here's to digitizing dreams and creating a brighter tomorrow.

With hope and purpose,
Digital warrior